# FRIENDLY PHYSICAL SCIENCE

Joey Hajda DVM MEd
Lisa B. Hajda MEd
Illustrated by Charlotte J. Hajda

STUDENT
WORKBOOK

Name_____ Date_____

Friendly Physical Science

## Lesson 1 Worksheet 1

Please fill in the missing words in each statement below. Refer back to your textbook for help.

1. Physical science is the study of those things in our world which are _____.

2. _____ is important in studying non-living things.

3. The distance from one point to another is known as _____.

4. Measuring something means we are comparing an unknown quantity to a _____ or known quantity.

5. Standards must be _____ by those persons using it.

6. The English system of measurement utilizes _____, _____ and miles as the standard of length measurement.

7. The metric system is known as the SI or _____.

8. The metric system relies on the standard units being in multiples of _____.

9. The base unit for length in the SI system is the _____.

10. The base unit for mass in the SI system is the _____.

11. The base unit for time in the SI system is the _____.

12. The metric prefix deci- refers to _____ of the base unit.

13. A decimeter is _____ of a meter.

14. The metric prefix centi- refers to _____ of the base unit.

15. A centimeter is _____ of a meter.

16. The metric prefix milli- refers to _____ of the base unit.

17. A millimeter is _____ of a meter.

18. The metric prefix deca- refers to _____ times the base unit.

19. A decameter equals _____ meters.

20. The metric prefix hecto- refers to _____ times the base unit.

21. A hectometer equals _____ meters.

22. The metric prefix kilo- refers to _____ times the base unit.

23. A kilometer equals _____ meters.

Name_____ Date_____

Friendly Physical Science

## Lesson 1 Worksheet 2

Below you will find 10 lines. Find the length of each line in the designated set of units.

1. _____ _____inches

2. _____ _____inches

3. _____ _____inches

4. _____ _____inches

5. _____ _____inch

6. _____
   _____cm

7. _____
   _____cm

8. _____
   _____cm

9. _____
   _____cm

10. _____ _____cm

Choose the best response to this question.

11. John had 40 decimeters of gold thread. Mary had 40 decameters of gold thread. Who had the longer piece of gold thread and why?

a. John had the longer piece because one decimeter is longer than one decameter.

b. John had the longer piece because one decameter is longer than one decimeter.

c. Mary had the longer piece because one decameter is longer than one decimeter.

d. Neither had a longer piece as one decimeter equals one decameter.

Name_____ Date_____

Friendly Physical Science

## Lesson 2 Worksheet 1

Please fill in the missing words in each statement below. Refer back to your textbook for help.

1. Measurements made when two or more base measurements are added, subtracted, multiplied or divided are known as _____ measurements.

2. The amount of space in a location is known as _____.

3. Surface area is a _____ dimensional measurment (derived from two measurements).

4. Floor tiles are usually _____ foot in length and width.

5. A floor tile measuring one foot in length and width is considered to have a surface area of _____.

6. A room in a house has the following floor dimensions: 20 feet by 25 feet. What is the area of the floor of the room in this house? _____.

7. Another room in the house has the following dimensions: 32 feet by 20 feet. What is the area of the floor in this room? _____.

8. A field measures 800 feet long and has a width of 200 feet. What is the area of this field? _____.

9. Suppose you have 20 cows and each cow requires 500 square feet of pasture. What is the total size of the pasture you would need for your herd of cows? _____.

10. Referring back to question 9, suppose one side of your pasture measured 50 feet. What must the other dimension be of the pasture to make sure all cows had enough area to graze? _____. Make a sketch of the pasture here if necessary to help you solve this question.

Name_____ Date_____

Friendly Physical Science

## Lesson 2 Worksheet 2

Tim and Sue had several cards in various sizes. Below you can see the measurements of these cards. Of the two cards given, choose who (Tim or Sue) had the card with the greater surface area. Write that person's name in the blank for each question.

1. Tim's card measured 6 inches by 5 inches. Sue's card measured 16 inches by 2 inches.
   _____ had the card with greater surface area.

2. Tim's card measured 6 inches by 3 inches. Sue's card measured 4 inches by 5 inches.
   _____ had the card with greater surface area.

3. Tim's card measured 16 inches by 5 inches. Sue's card measured 9 inches by 8 inches.
   _____ had the card with greater surface area.

4. Tim's card measured 2.5 inches by 4 inches. Sue's card measured 3 inches by 3 inches.
   _____ had the card with greater surface area.

5. Tim's card measured 72 inches by 5 inches. Sue's card measured 9 inches by 40 inches.
   _____ had the card with greater surface area.

Take a look at the box pictured here. What would be the total surface area of this box? Write the area of each surface in the spaces below. Then find the total surface area of the box.

6. Side A = _____
7. Side B = _____
8. Side C = _____
9. Side D = _____
10. Side E = _____
11. Side F = _____
12. Total surface area = _____
13. Would a 150 cm² piece of paper cover this box?
_____

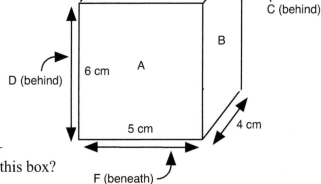

Name_____ Date_____

Friendly Physical Science

## Lesson 3 Worksheet 1

Please fill in the missing words in each statement below. Refer back to your textbook for help.

1. The amount of space something takes up in known as its _____.

2. Volume is a _____ measurement (base or derived?)

3. To find the volume of a regularly-shaped object, one must use the base measurement of _____.

4. A regularly-shaped object has surfaces which are _____.

5. In order to find the volume of a regularly-shaped object one must first find the _____ of the bottom or base of the object.

6. After finding the area of the base of the object, this value is multiplied by the _____ of the object.

7. Volume measurements of regularly-shaped objects are in _____ units or units$^3$.

8. The "formula" for finding the volume of a regularly-shaped object, therefore, is to multiply the _____ times the _____ times the _____ of the object.

Examine each regularly-shaped object below. Find the volume of each.

9. _____

10. _____

11. _____

12. _____

9. (5 cm × 4 cm × 3 cm)

10. (11 cm × 2 cm × 2 cm)

11. (10 cm × 4 cm × 5 cm)

12. (3 cm, 6 cm, 2 cm, 8 cm, 8 cm)

Name_____ Date_____

Friendly Physical Science

## Lesson 3 Worksheet 2

There are ten regularly-shaped objects below.  Match each shape to its measured volume.

1. Shape letter _____ = ___64 cm$^3$___
2. Shape letter _____ = ___252 cm$^3$___
3. Shape letter _____ = ___216 cm$^3$___
4. Shape letter _____ = __105 cm$^3$___
5. Shape letter _____ = ___175 cm$^3$__
6. Shape letter _____ = _175 cm$^3$
7. Shape letter _____ = _72 cm$^3$_
8. Shape letter _____ = _36 cm$^3$__
9. Shape letter _____ = _100 cm$^3$__
10. Shape letter _____ = 90 cm$^3$

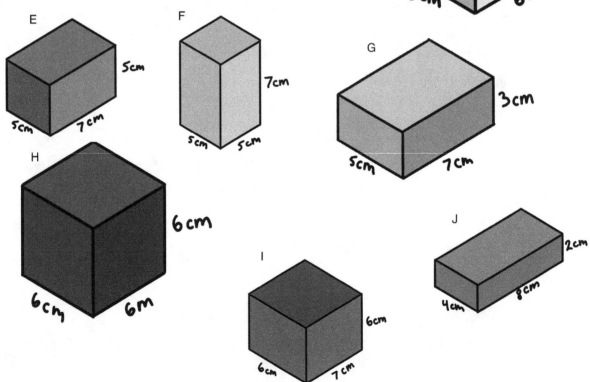

Name_____ Date_____

Friendly Physical Science

## Lesson 4 Worksheet 1

Please fill in the missing words in each statement below. Refer back to your textbook for help.

1. _____ is a measure of how much space an object occupies.

2. Volume is a _____ dimensional measurement.

3. An irregularly-shaped object has surfaces which are not _____.

4. To find the volume of an irregularly-shaped object we can use the _____ method.

5. With regard to the displacement method of finding volume, the _____ of water displaced by the object equals the _____ of the object.

6. The SI unit for volume of an irregularly-shaped object is the _____.

7. A liter can be divided into 1000 equal parts. Each of these "little" parts are known as _____.

8. An instrument often used to find the volume of a liquid is the _____ cylinder.

9. A milliliter of water equals 1 _____ of water.

10. Syringes often measure liquids in _____ (units).

11. The upper surface of a liquid placed into a graduated cylinder is _____ in shape. This curve is known as the _____.

12. The rule to reading the volume of a liquid in a gradutaed cylinder it to read the _____ of the meniscus.

13. _____ quarts are found in one gallon.

14. _____ cups are found in one pint.

15. _____ pints are found in one quart.

16. One cup contains _____ ounces.

17. _____ teaspoons are found in one Tablespoon.

18. _____ cups are found in one gallon.

19. _____ cups are found in four gallons.

20. Ten tablespoons are found in _____ ounces.

7

Name_____Date_____

Friendly Physical Science

## Lesson 4 Worksheet 2

Read each secnario below and tell which of the two objects being measured is the larger of the two.

1. A container of water was filled to the 100 mL level. Object A was dropped in and the water rose to 150 mL. Object A was removed from the container. The water was refilled to the 90 mL level and the water rose to 130 mL when Object B was dropped in. Which object was the larger of the two?

_____

2. A container of water was filled to the 110 mL level. Object A was dropped in and the water rose to 115 mL. Object A was removed from the container. The water was refilled to the 120 mL level and the water rose to 130 mL when Object B was dropped in. Which object was the larger of the two?

_____

3. A container of water was filled to the 150 mL level. Object A was dropped in and the water rose to 185 mL. Object A was removed from the container. The water was refilled to the 110 mL level and the water rose to 145 mL when Object B was dropped in. Which object was the larger of the two?

_____

4. A container of water was filled to the 125 mL level. Object A was dropped in and the water rose to 150 mL. Object A was removed from the container. The water was refilled to the 90 mL level and the water rose to 130 mL when Object B was dropped in. Which object was the larger of the two?

_____

Name_____ Date_____

Friendly Physical Science

## Lesson 5 Worksheet

(Note: there is only one worksheet for Lesson 5)

Please fill in the missing words in each statement below. Refer back to your textbook for help.

1. Mass the the amount of _____ in an object.

2. Mass and weight are not the same thing. This is a _____ statement (true or false).

3. Matter consists of small bits known as _____.

4. Weight is dependent upon _____.

5. An object's mass on the earth will _____ change if it goes to the moon.

6. An object's weight _____ change if it goes to a location where gravity is not the same.

7. The mass of an object is measured using a _____ or a _____.

8. The SI units for mass are _____.

9. One thousand grams equal one _____.

10. One one-thousandth of a gram equals one _____.

11. The English measurement for mass is the _____.

12. One pound equals _____ dry ounces.

13. There are _____ grams in one pound.

14. One ton equals _____ pounds.

15. A metric ton equals _____ kilograms.

9

Name_____ Date_____

Friendly Physical Science

## Lesson 6 Worksheet 1

Please fill in the missing words in each statement below. Refer back to your textbook for help.

1. _____ is the amount of matter that can be found in a unit of volume.

2. The unit of volume usually associated with a density measurement is the _____.

3. Density is a _____ measurement (base or derived).

4. To find the density of an object one must first measure its _____ and then its _____.

5. Lead fishing weights will have a _____ density when compared to cotton balls.

6. If the object in which you would like to find the density is a regularly-shaped object, you could find its volume by _____.

7. If the object in which you would like to find the density is an irregularly-shaped object, you could find its volume using the _____ method.

8. To find the mass of an object, you could use a _____ or _____.

9. The units for density would be _____ per _____.

10. The density of pure water is _____.

11. Substances with a density greater than that of water will _____ when placed into water.

12. Substances with a density less than that of water will _____ when placed into water.

13. Density can be used to _____ substances.

14. Liquids, with varying _____ will separate, too.

15. The property of density can also be used to _____ substances.

Name_____ Date_____

Friendly Physical Science

## Lesson 6 Worksheet 2

Francis had six unidentified pieces of metal. She thought that if she could determine the density of each piece, she might be able to figure out the identity of each piece using a reference book which told the accepted density of metals. She tested each piece of metal and took the average mass and volume. Those results are listed below. At the bottom of the page is a reference chart which tells accepted densities of various metals. Using Francis' results and the chart below, tell what you think the identity is for each unknown metal.

Sample 1: Mass 27.0 g  Volume 10 cc  Identity: _____

Sample 2: Mass 44.5 g  Volume 5 cc  Identity: _____

Sample 3: Mass 70.8 g  Volume 12 cc  Identity: _____

Sample 4: Mass 183.4 g  Volume 9.5 cc  Identity: _____

Sample 5: Mass 215 g  Volume 10 mL  Identity: _____

Sample 6: Mass 147 g  Volume 14 mL  Identity: _____

Metal Densities:

Aluminum: 2.7 g/cc   Lead: 11.3 g/cc   Copper: 8.96 g/cc   Gallium: 5.91 g/cc
Cesium: 1.93 g/cc   Silver: 10.5 g/cc   Gold: 19.3 g/cc   Platinum: 21.5 g/cc
Titanium: 4.5 g/cc   Zinc: 7.41 g/cc

Name_____Date_____

Friendly Physical Science

## Lesson 7 Worksheet

(Note: there is only one worksheet for Lesson 7)

Please fill in the missing words in each statement below. Refer back to your textbook for help.

1. Objects which have a density greater than that of water will _____ when placed into water.

2. Objects which have a density less than that of water will _____ when placed into water.

3. The force which allows objects to float that would otherwise sink based upon their density is known as _____.

4. Increasing the volume of water being displaced while keeping the mass of an object constant can have the effect of reducing that object's _____ thereby enabling it to float.

5. Tommy has two boats: Boat A has a volume of 500 cc. Boat B has a volume of 600 cc. The mass of each boat is 400 grams. Which boat will float, A or B, both or neither?

_____

Name_____ Date_____

Friendly Physical Science

## Lesson 8 Worksheet

(Note: there is only one worksheet for Lesson 8)

Please fill in the missing words in each statement below. Refer back to your textbook for help.

1. _____ is defined as the ability or capacity to do work.

2. Work is defined as a change in _____ of an object which has mass.

3. Energy can be present in various forms such as: _____, _____, _____, _____ or nuclear.

4. _____ energy is stored energy or energy "waiting" to do work.

5. _____ energy is the energy of motion.

6. A shining light bulb could be an example of _____ or _____ energy.

7. A pump with handle that can be moved up and down is an example of using _____ energy to do work.

8. A beating drum creates _____ energy.

9. Mixing various chemicals together can potentially produce _____ energy.

10. Burning wood produces _____ energy.

11. True or False: Energy can be converted from one type to another. _____

12. A compressed spring is an example of _____ energy.

13. A released spring flying through the air is an example of _____ energy having been converted into _____ energy.

14. Water held behind a dam is an example of _____ energy.

15. Water flowing through an outlet of a dam causing a turbine to turn is an example of potential energy being converted into _____ energy.

13

Name_____ Date_____

Friendly Physical Science

## Lesson 9 Worksheet 1

Please fill in the missing words in each statement below. Refer back to your textbook for help.

1. The base unit for time is the _____.

2. _____ seconds equals one minute.

3. _____ minutes or _____ seconds equals one hour.

4. _____ seconds or _____ minutes or _____ hours equals one day.

5. Speed can be defined as the _____ it takes to travel a specific _____.

6. The mathematical formula for speed is _____.

7. The speed at which an automobile travels is usually measured in _____ in the US.

8. _____ is also a measure of speed but it also includes the direction of travel.

9. A change in the rate of speed is known as _____.

10. Speeding up is known as _____ acceleration while slowing down is referred to as _____ acceleration.

Name_____ Date_____

Friendly Physical Science

## Lesson 9 Worksheet 2

Here are some story problems related to speed. Read each one carefully.

1. Tony traveled a distance of 500 feet on his bike in 40 seconds. How many feet per second was he traveling? _____

2. Marcus shot a bottle rocket into the sky. If it traveled 30 meters in three seconds, what as the speed of the rocket? _____

3. Hank traveled 50 meters in 5 seconds. Marcia traveled 100 meters in 10 seconds. Who had the greater speed? _____

4. Suppose you were in your car traveling at a speed of 60 miles per hour. If you were able to maintain that speed constantly for three hours, how far could you theoreticallly travel?
_____

5. Mary was slowing down to make a left turn at a street intersection. Initially, she was traveling at 35 miles/hour. At the point of the turn, she was now travling at a speed of 10 miles/hour. Was Mary experiencing positive or negative acceleration as she made the turn?
_____

Name_____ Date_____

Friendly Physical Science

## Lesson 10 Worksheet 1

Please fill in the missing words in each statement below.  Refer back to your textbook for help.

1. Newton's three laws of motion can be credited to _____, however _____ and _____ had also made contributions to many of these ideas.

2. Newtons first law of motion states that an object in _____ remains _____ in a _____ line until acted upon by another _____.

3. The force which could possibly be applied may change the object's _____ of travel or _____ of travel.

4. Newton's first law applies also to objects at _____ in that an object at _____ will remain at _____ until acted upon by another force.

5. The term which describes objects in regard to Newton's first law is _____.

6. Newton's second law of motion tells of the relationship between _____, _____ and _____.

7. Essentially, Newton's second law of motion says that as a force is applied to an object, its potential _____ will be amplified.

8. Newton's third law of motion states for every _____ there is an equal, but opposite _____.

9. Good examples of Newton's third law include _____ a boat or walking across a _____.

10. The _____ in your car is a great example of how an object can apply a force to a moving object which results in a change in acceleration of that object.

Name_____ Date_____

Friendly Physical Science

## Lesson 10 Worksheet 2

Below are some "thinking" type questions. Read each question carefully and ALL possible responses. Choose the one best response to each question.

1. Harrison and Sheila were traveling on a gokart at a speed of 40 mph. Suddenly a rabbit ran out onto the gokart track in front of the two and Harrison hit the brakes very hard. Both Harrison and Sheila moved quite far forward onto the edge of the seat before their seatbelts applied a force to them. Why did they move forward even though the gokart was coming to a stop?

a. Both Harrison and Sheila were in motion before the rabbit ran out. The rabbit applied a magnetic force to the two causing them to move forward.

b. Both Harrison and Sheila were at rest in the car when the rabbit ran out in front of them. The braking of the gokart caused them to move forward.

c. Harrison and Sheila were both in motion when the brakes were being applied. They continued in motion according to Newton's first law of motion until the seatbelts applied a force to stop them.

d. Harrison and Sheila applied a force to the rabbit using the brakes of the car to teach it a lesson to not run across the road.


2. Marty was flying in an airplane for the very first time to visit his grandparents. As the plane was taking off, Marty felt his head and body being pressed into the seat, but later it lessened as the plane moved into the air. Why did this happen?

a. Marty was traveling at a slow speed as the plane taxied on the airstrip just before the plane quickly accelerated to a much faster speed for takeoff. His body desired to stay at the initial speed, but because the plane applied a greater force through the seat, he was moved into the seat.

b. Air in front of Marty quickly forced him to move forward to allow the plane to speed up for takeoff.

c. Marty's seat applied an upward force just before takeoff through a potential energy system found in the springs of the seat.

d. The force being applied to Marty cannot be explained.

3. Lisa and her friends liked to ride the super fast roller coasters at amusement parks. They loved the thrill of suddenly going down a steep hill but knew it was important to not have any loose objects with them in the car of the roller coaster. Why is this important?

a. Newton's first law applies to all objects moving in the roller coaster car. A sudden turn or drop could result in those objects continuing in a straight line and being hurled out of the car.

b. Loose objects can make it difficult to keep one's feet firmly planted in the car of the roller coaster.

c. Newton's first law says that objects in motion always stop being in motion no matter how fast they are going to being with.

d. It's easy to hold onto loose objects while riding on a roller coaster, so it's always okay to just set them beside you on the seat and enjoy the ride.


4. Large semitrucks are often used to haul cattle to and from pastures or feedlots and slaughterhouses. The cattle are placed into large trailers, many times in two layers. The total weight of the cattle can often exceed 50,000 pounds. Which factor below must be considered when hauling such large loads of objects which are not using seatbelts?

a. Drivers must be careful to apply brakes slowly and in plenty of time to stop at intersections. Otherwise cattle may suddenly lurch forward causing the driver to have difficulty stopping the truck.

b. Drivers must be careful to make turns gradually at speeds much slower than in a personal automobile.

c. Drivers must be aware that the livestock can readily shift in position at unexpected times which may cause him to potentially lose control of the truck.

d. All of these factors are important to consider when hauling objects which can readily move around in a trailer.

Name_____ Date_____

Friendly Physical Science

## Lesson 11 Worksheet 1

Please fill in the missing words in each statement below. Refer back to your textbook for help.

1. _____ is defined as the movement of an object through the action of a force.

2. _____ allow us to do work on objects with less effort. They, in effect, "do" work for us.

3. _____ are simple machines which consist of a straight bar or rod and a fulcrum.

4. The _____ is the point on which the bar or rod moves.

5. The rod or bar of a lever can be divided into two parts: the _____ arm and the _____ arm.

6. The effort arm of a lever is where a force is _____ while the load arm is where a force is applied to an _____.

7. Levers can be placed into three different _____ based upon where the _____ is located.

8. A lever where the fulcrum is placed between the effort arm and the load arm is classified as a _____ class lever.

9. In a first class lever, the direction of the effort force is _____ that of the load force. In other words, if one presses down on a first class lever, the object being moved goes _____.

10. The magnification of a force using a simple machine is known as _____ _____.

11. To increase the mechanical advantage of a first class lever, one can either _____ the effort arm or _____ the load arm.

12. A _____ class lever has the fulcrum beyond both the effort and load arms.

13. With a second class lever, both the _____ force and the _____ force move in the same _____.

14. A _____ is an example of a second class lever that was used by Native Americans before the advent of wheeled carts or wagons.

15. Both class _____ and class _____ levers provide a mechanical advantage for the user, but the distance the object is moved is less than that of the effort distance.

More on the next page.

16. The _____ force is applied _____ the fulcrum and the load in a third class lever sytem.

17. A third class lever system does not provide a _____ for the user. Instead, it works to _____ the speed of motion of the object upon which the force is being applied.

18. A _____ used to sweep or an _____ used to paddle with are great examples of third class levers.

19. When levers are designed to work together, the force being applied is _____ from one lever to the next.

20. A _____ used to cut bolts, heavy chains or locks is a great example of using multiple levers to make very difficult job very easy.

Name_____Date_____

Friendly Physical Science

## Lesson 11 Worksheet 2

Below are some simple lever designs. Answer the questions about each of these designs to the best of your ability.

1. If a load is placed at point B and an effort force is applied downward at point A, in which direction will the load move?

a. up

b. down

c. left

d. north


2. If the load remains at point B, at what point would one gain the greatest mechanical advantage using this system?

a. A

b. B

c. C

d. D


3. If the load were moved to point D on the lever, would be force to lift the load become easier or more difficult

a. Easier

b. More difficult

c. It would remain the same


4. Would moving the fulcrum closer to point B (assuming the load is at point B) make it easier or more difficult to lift the load at point B?

a. Yes, easier

b. No, not easier

5. Assume a load is placed at point D on this lever and an effort force is applied in an upward direction at point A. Will the load move up or down?

a. Up

b. Down

c. It won't move at all.


6. Which class of lever would this system depict?

a. First class lever

b. Second class lever

c. Third class lever

d. Science class lever


7. To make the job of lifting an object using this system eaiser, which position would be the best to lift an object, point C, D or B?

a. C

b. D

c. B

d. it doesn't matter

Name_____ Date_____

Friendly Physical Science

## Lesson 12 Worksheet 1

Please fill in the missing words in each statement below. Refer back to your textbook for help.

1. The _____ and _____ consists of two circular, disk-shaped objects that are joined together.

2. Of the two components, the wheel has the _____ diameter while the axle has the _____ diameter.

3. As the _____ turns so does the wheel.

4. The greater the difference in the diameter of the two components, the greater the _____ of the wheel and axle system.

5. When an effort force is applied to the _____ component of the wheel and axle system, a mechanical advantage is realized.

6. An example of this arrangement is the _____ in a car.

7. It's much _____ to change the direction of travel in a car by using the steering wheel while compared to just turning the bolt to which the steering wheel is attached.

8. Another example of this arrangement of wheel and axle is in the steering system of _____ where the wheel is used to adjust the rudder.

9. When an effort force is applied to the axle component in a wheel and axle system, the mechanical advantage realized is less than _____ .

10. This means that there is _____ work gained when applying a force to the axle of the wheel and axle system compared to when an effort force is applied to the wheel.

11. The advantage of applying a force to the axle component of a wheel and axle system is that the _____ of rotation the wheel is greater than that of the axle.

Name_____Date_____

Friendly Physical Science

## Lesson 12 Worksheet 2

Examine each set of wheel and axle systems below. Assume the effort force is being applied to the wheel in the system. Choose which of the two would provide the greatest mechanical advantage.

1. A.    B.

2. A. 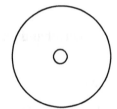   B.

3. A.    B.

4. A. 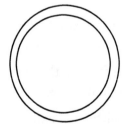   B.

Look at each wheel and axle system here. Assume the effort force is being appied to the axle. In which system would the wheel turn faster with one turn of the axle?

A. 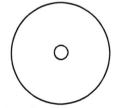   B.

24

Name_____ Date_____

Friendly Physical Science

## Lesson 13 Worksheet 1

Please fill in the missing words in each statement below. Refer back to your textbook for help.

1. A_____ is similar to the wheel and axle simple machine in that it consists of a wheel and axle.

2. However, with a pulley, the wheel is _____ attached to the axle. It, instead, _____ freely on the axle.

3. The wheel portion of a pulley has a groove on which a _____ or _____ can pass.

4. Pulleys allow one to _____ the _____ of the force being applied to the object. If using a single fixed pulley, pulling _____ will move the object upward.

5. A single fixed pulley allows one to _____ the direction of force, however, it does not create any _____ advantage for the user.

6. A single, non-fixed pulley with its _____ ropes or chains supporting the object can create a mechanical advantage of _____ for the user.

7. By _____ more pulleys to a system of pulleys one can greatly increase the _____ of the system. The user's force can be _____ many times.

8. A system of pulleys working side-by-side with a corresponding set of pulleys is known as a _____ and _____.

9. The number of ropes or chains supporting the object in a block and tackle system tells you the _____ of the system.

10. For example, if you had four ropes supporting the object in a block and tackle system, the mechanical advantage would be _____.

11. One disadvantage of a block and tackle system is that it requires _____ _____ of rope or chain to lift an object. To combat this issue, this rope or chain can be "recycled" back into the system.

12. Pulleys can be joined together with other pulleys through the use of _____ or _____. An example of this would be under the hood of your _____ where _____ transfer energy from the engine to other components requiring energy.

More on next page.

13. Pulleys that are joined through the use of belts or chains can _____ the _____ of the force being applied.  In other words, a clockwise rotation can be converted to a _____ rotation.

14. Pulleys that are joined through the use of belts of chains can also change the _____ of rotation.   A great example of this is a bike with several "speeds."

15. And, finally, pulleys that are joined together by a chain or belt can also be used to change the _____ of force one applies to the system.

16. _____ are basically pulleys which have notched surfaces which match one another and come into contact with each other.

17. Like sets of pulleys linked with belts or chains, gears can also change the _____ of the force being applied, change the amount of the _____ being applied or change the _____ at which the initial gear is being turned.

Name_____ Date_____

Friendly Physical Science

## Lesson 13 Worksheet 2

Look at the systems of pulleys below. Answer the questions associated with each system.

1. What is the mechanical advantage of this pulley system?

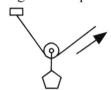

2. What is the mechanical advantage of this pulley system?

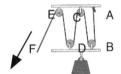

3. If pulley A is turning clockwise, what direction will pulley B turn?

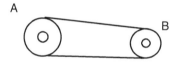

4. If pulley A is turning clockwise, what direction will pulley C turn?

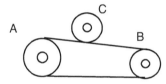

5. If pulley A makes one rotation, will pulley B make more or less rotations than pulley A?

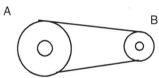

6. If a force is being applied to sprocket A, will there be a mechanical advantage realized at sprocket B?

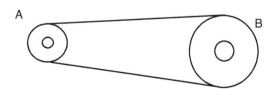

Name_____  Date_____

Friendly Physical Science

## Lesson 14 Worksheet 1

Please fill in the missing words in each statement below. Refer back to your textbook for help.

1. An _____ is a flat surface (plane) which has been raised or lifted on one end.

2. The mechanical advantage of a ramp is related to the _____ of the ramp (the run) and the _____ of the ramp (the rise).

3. The longer the run of a ramp, the _____ the mechanical advantage of the ramp.

4. A _____ is two inclined planes matched together.

5. Wedges are capable of changing the _____ being applied to the wedge.

6. The resulting direction of force is _____ to the initial force.

7. The mechanical advantage of a wedge is related to the _____ of the wedge and the _____ along the narrow edge of the wedge.

8. A _____ is an inclined plane wrapped into a circular shape. Screws and bolts convert _____ motion into _____ motion and, along with _____, can hold objects together.

9. An _____ is a screw which turns inside a cylinder and can be used to lift substances.

10. _____ is the reluctance of substances to move across each other when they are rubbed together.

Name_____ Date_____

Friendly Physical Science

## Lesson 14 Worksheet 2

Look at the systems of inclined planes below. Answer the question about each system.

1. Which ramp would provide the greater mechanical advantage?

2. Which ramp would provide the greater mechanical advantage?

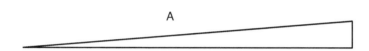 

3. Which wedge would make your job easier?

 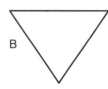

4. If this screw were turned in a clockwise direction, would it move into or out of this piece of wood?

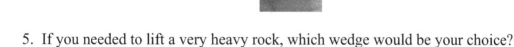

5. If you needed to lift a very heavy rock, which wedge would be your choice?

6. If this wedge were to be used to split this log, draw an arrow indicating the initial direction of force of the wedge and the resulting direction of force as it acted upon the log.

29

Name_____Date_____

Friendly Physical Science

## Lesson 15 Worksheet 1

Please fill in the missing words in each statement below. Refer back to your textbook for help.

1. _____ can be defined as a force acting in a perpendicular direction to a surface over a specific _____.

2. Pressure is measured in SI units known as _____ (Pa). A pascal is defined as one _____ of force acting upon one _____ of area.

3. Pressure = _____/area. Pressure is the amount of _____ per unit of area.

4. Liquids are very _____ to compress, however, gases can _____ be compressed.

5. When pressure is applied to a liquid or gas that is in a closed container, the pressure is _____ distributed to all parts of the substance and therefore the pressure is equally felt upon all surfaces of the container.

6. A mechanical advantage can be realized by adjusting the _____ upon which a pressure is acting in multi-cylinder systems.

7. An increase in mechanical advantage of a pressurized cylinder system comes at the cost of _____ _____ traveled by second cylinder of the system.

8. Systems which utlilze liquids to transfer forces through hoses and cylinders are known as _____ systems.

9. Systems which utilze gases to transfer forces through hoses and cylinders are known as _____ systems.

10. _____ systems tend to exhibit a "gentler" start at actuation while _____ tend to be more abrupt at actuation of the system.

Name_____Date_____

Friendly Physical Science

## Lesson 15 Worksheet 1

Examine each pressure system below. Answer the question found with each system.

1. Cylinder A has a surface area of 4 cm². Cylinder B has a surface area of 8 cm². Will actuating Cylinder A provide a mechanical advantage for the user? If so, how much?

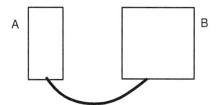

2. Cylinder A has a surface area of 4 cm². Cylinder B has a surface area of 16 cm². Will actuating Cylinder A provide a mechanical advantage for the user? If so, how much?

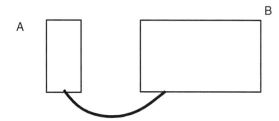

3. Cylinder A has a surface area of 4 cm². Cylinder B has a surface area of 2 cm². Will actuating Cylinder A provide a mechanical advantage for the user? If so, how much?

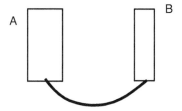

4. Suppose you wanted to utilize a hydraulic system to move a lever a great distance by moving the control lever only a short distance. Would you want the second cylinder to have larger or smaller diameter than the control lever? Why?

Name_____ Date_____

Friendly Physical Science

## Lesson 16 Worksheet

(Note that Lesson 16 has only one worksheet.)

Please fill in the missing words in each statement below. Refer back to your textbook for help.

1. _____ is thought to occur due to unidirectional spins of _____ in magnetic substances.

2. The term unidirectional means _____.

3. Magnets create three-dimensional _____ _____ about them.

4. "Like" magnetic poles of a magnet _____ each other.

5. "Unlike" magnetic poles _____ each other.

6. Non-magnetic substances can be _____ by rubbing magnets across them in the same direction.

7. These types of magnets usually don't last very long and are called _____.

8. Magnets which maintain their ability to attract or repel over long periods of time are known as _____ magnets.

9. The earth has a _____ _____ about it.

10. The magnetized needle in a _____ aligns itself with these fields and points in a _____-_____ direction.


Look at these situations below. Tell if the magnets will attract or repel each other.

11. [N    S]  [N    S]   _____

12. [S    N]  [N    S]   _____

13. [S    N]  [S    N]   _____

14. [N    S]  [S    N]   _____

Name_____ Date_____

Friendly Physical Science

## Lesson 17 Worksheet 1

Please fill in the missing words in each statement below. Refer back to your textbook for help.

1. The movement of _____ between atoms or through objects is electricity.

2. _____ electricity is movement of electrons across relatively short distances.

3. _____ electricity is movement of electrons across long distances.

4. Current electricity is in two forms: _____ current and _____ current electricity.

5. Direct current electricity is created by _____ or _____ _____ and flows in _____ direction.

6. Alternating current electricity is created by _____ and travels in an alternating _____ and _____ direction.

7. _____ electricity is more of a nuisance, yet must be respected regarding safety issues.

8. Electricity desires to ground into the _____.

9. _____ rods redirect lightning discharges into the _____ away from building and home structures.

10. _____ create electricity through the reaction of two unlike _____ and an _____.

11. Electrons travel with ease through _____ and with much greater difficulty through _____.

12. _____, especially copper and aluminum, are very good conductors.

13. Current, measured in _____, is the _____ at which electrical charges travel.

14. Voltage, measured in _____, is the relative _____ of the charges.

15. Resistance, measured in _____, is the degree to which electrons find it difficult to travel through substances.

16. Watts is a measure of _____ provided by the electrical circuit and is a derived measurement of _____ times _____.

17. Household circuits utilize _____ volt _____ circuits.

18. Car batteries are usually _____ volt DC circuits.

19. _____ and _____ switches allow safe levels of electricity to supply electrical outlets in our homes.

33

Name_____ Date_____

Friendly Physical Science

## Lesson 17 Worksheet 2

Please tell whether the statement below about electricity is true or false.

1. _____ Electricity is the flow of protons through substances.

2. _____ Current electricity is what you see when you receive a shock after sliding your feet across a carpet.

3. _____ DC electricity comes from generators and what is used in most homes.

4. _____ Insulators are substances which resist the flow of electricity.

5. _____ Lightning is an example of static electricity and can be deadly.

6. _____ Batteries work through the chemical reaction of an acid and two unlike metals.

7. _____ The speed at which electricity is flowing is known as current and is measured in amperes.

8. _____ Resistance to the flow of electricity is measured in ohms.

9. _____ Alternating current electricity moves back and forth as it travels away from the battery which produces it.

10. _____ Water, held behind a dam, can convert its potential energy into mechanical and ultimately electrical energy through the use of turbines inside the dam.

11. _____ Fuses and breaker switches are safety devices which prevent the excess flow of electricity through a circuit.

Name_____ Date_____

Friendly Physical Science

## Lesson 18 Worksheet

(Note that Lesson 18 has only one worksheet.)

Please fill in the missing words in each statement below. Refer back to your textbook for help.

1. _____ _____ are produced around wires that are carrying electricity.

2. Coils of wires, carrying _____ _____, alongside a soft iron core creates an electromagnet.

3. Electromagnets are _____ magnets meaning they only function while electrical current is flowing.

4. A _____ allows one to control when an electromagnet is functioning and when it is not.

5. The _____ of an electromagnet can be reversed by reversing the flow of electricity.

6. With an electromagnet being controlled by a battery, one simply has to _____ the connections on the battery to change the polarity of the magnet.

7. A combination of _____ magnets and _____ with changing polarity allow electric motors to work.

8. Bringing the positive end of an electromagnet near the positive end of a permanent magnet will cause the two magnets to _____ each other.

9. The biggest advantage of an electromagnet over a permanent magnet is that electromagnets can be turned _____ and _____ at the user's convenience.

10. _____ are coils of wire which act upon moveable rods found within.

11. Common uses for solenoids include: _____, _____ and _____.

12. To increase the strength of an electromagnet one can either increase the _____ of coils or increase the flow of _____.

13. Look at the diagram below and tell whether the electromagnet within this motor will rotate or stay in this position.

Name_____ Date_____

Friendly Physical Science

## Lesson 19 Worksheet 1

Please fill in the missing words in each statement below. Refer back to your textbook for help.

1. The source of natural light in our world comes from the _____.

2. Man-made light comes from _____.

3. Light is defined as the _____ of electromagnetic radiation which have the capability of traveling from place to place.

4. Light travels at approximately _____ miles per second or _____ miles per hour.

5. Light that we can see is part of the _____ spectrum.

6. Light travels in _____ with varying wavelengths.

7. Colors of light are dependent upon the _____ of the light.

8. _____ we can observe are the light which has reflected from an object.

9. A _____ can be used to separate light into the spectrum of wavelengths.

10. Refraction is the _____ of light as it moves into different substances.

11. _____ are used to bend light rays which enables images to be focused.

12. _____ is the bouncing-off of light from a surface.

13. With regard to reflection, the angle of _____ equals the angle of _____ .

14. Solar energy can be used to create _____ through the use of silicon-filled photovoltaic cells.

15. This DC electricity can then be stored in _____ for later use.

Name_____   Date_____

Friendly Physical Science

## Lesson 19 Worksheet 2

Examine each diagram below. Label the indicated parts or provide the requested value.

PARTS OF A WAVE

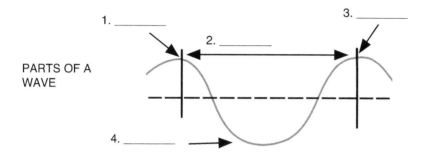

1. _____
2. _____
3. _____
4. _____

STRUCTURES OF THE EYE

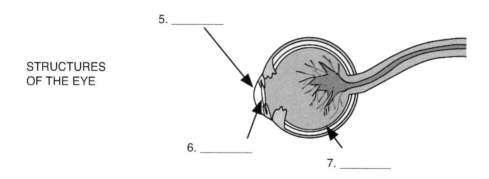

5. _____
6. _____
7. _____

ANGLES OF INCIDENCE AND REFLECTION

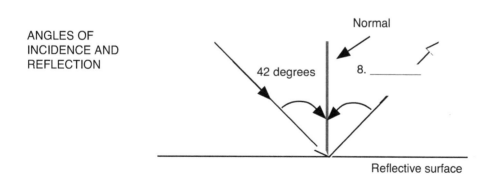

8. _____

37

Name_____ Date_____

Friendly Physical Science

## Lesson 20 Worksheet

(Note: there is only one worksheet for Lesson 20)

Please fill in the missing words in each statement below. Refer back to your textbook for help.

1. Sound energy, which travels in _____, is defined as audible changes in _____ (vibrations) which can travel through a medium such as air.

2. Sounds are described as having a range of _____ with high frequencies being _____ pitched tones and low frequencies being _____ pitched tones.

3. Humans can hear a certain _____ of frequencies while animals can hear frequencies above and below that of humans.

4. Sounds travels much _____ than light only going at _____ miles per hour.

5. Light travels _____ miles per hour.

6. Sound travels _____ through water than air and yet, even faster through _____ substances.

7. _____ (very high frequency sound) is used in health diagnosis and for prenatal care.

8. Loudness of sound is measured in _____.

10. True or False: Loud noises, over long periods of time, generally do no harm to our ears.


Use the chart in your lesson to rate these sounds from softest (1) to loudest (7).

_____ Quiet office

_____ Soft radio

_____ Rustling leaves

_____ Night club

_____ Live rock band

_____ Normal piano practice

_____ Cymbal crash

Name_____ Date_____

Friendly Physical Science

## Lesson 21 Worksheet

(Note: there is only one worksheet for Lesson 21)

Please fill in the missing words in each statement below. Refer back to your textbook for help.

1. All substances contain _____ held in their atoms.

2. There are four phases of matter: _____, _____, _____ and plasma.

3. Solids have the _____ amount of energy, liquids have _____, gases even more and plasma the most energy.

4. Adding heat energy to substances allow them to change _____.

5. The temperature at which a solid changes to a liquid is known as the _____.

6. The temperature at which a liquid changes to a gas is known as the _____ point or evaporation point.

7. There are three commonly used systems of measuring temperature (heat content) of a substance: _____, _____ and _____.

8. Zero degrees Kelvin is known as _____ zero where all action of atoms in a substance _____.

9. In general, substances _____ when heated and _____ when cooled.

10. Heat moves through our environment by _____, convection or _____.

11. Movement by conduction occurs when heat energy travels _____ a substance.

12. Movement by _____ occurs due to the heating of liquids or gases which change density and create movement of those substances to other locations.

13. Movement by _____ is through travel of infrared radiation and travels in all _____ from the source.

14. Unlike other substances, water _____ upon freezing.

15. Water has a great capacity to absorb _____ without increasing in _____.

Name_____Date_____

Friendly Physical Science

## Lesson 22 Worksheet

(Note: there is only one worksheet for Lesson 22)

Please fill in the missing words in each statement below. Refer back to your textbook for help.

1. 1. All things, whether living or non-living consist of tiny bits of matter known as _____.

2. The central portion of an atom is known as the _____ and it contains subatomic particles known as the _____ and the_____.

3. Circling around the nucleus of the atom are a third type of subatomic particle which are the _____.

4. Theories say it is the _____ of the electrons which determines the behavior of various elements on the periodic table.

5. To determine the number of protons or electrons an atom of a particular atom has, one looks for the _____ of that element on a periodic table.

6. The electrons are thought to exist in _____ around the nucleus of an atom and that there can be no more than _____ on one of these layers.

7. Elements which have their outermost layer of electrons filled are the elements which are very _____ in their behavior.

8. Elements which have their outermost layers incompletely filled are elements which are very _____ in their behavior.

9. Elements which are very reactive seek to gain stability by moving or sharing _____ with neighboring atoms of elements.

10. The family of elements whose atoms have their outer layers of electrons completely filled making their very, very stable is the _____ family.

11. Atomic bonds which form between atoms who have transferred electrons from one to another are known as _____ bonds.

12. Atomic bonds which form between atoms who are sharing electrons between themselves

are known as _____ bonds.

13. Of the many elements known to man, there are four that are common to all living things. Those four elements are: _____, _____, _____ and _____. Write their element symbols next to their names, too!

14. Of the elements listed below, choose the one that would most likely be the least reactive.

A. Hydrogen

B. Carbon

C. Sodium

D. Neon

15. Of the elements listed below, choose the one that would most likely be the most reactive.

A. Neon

B. Sodium

C. Argon

D. Helium

16. Which subatomic particle is thought to be responsible for an atom's behavior?

A. Proton

B. Neutron

C. Electron

D. Crouton

17. Suppose Atom A desires to get rid of one electron and Atom B is willing to accept that one electron. Together, by moving this electron, they can become a compound which is stable. This type of bond formation where electrons are moved is called a(n)

A. Proton bond

B. Single covalent bond

C. Double covalent bond

D. Ionic bond

E. James bond (LOL)

CPSIA information can be obtained
at www.ICGtesting.com
Printed in the USA
BVHW010030011019
559816BV00003BA/51/P